——Projects

Untitled Projects

SLOPE

by pamela carter

This production of *Slope* was first performed at the
Citizens Circle Studio, Glasgow, on 12 November 2014

SLOPE

by pamela carter

PAUL	Owen Whitelaw
MATHILDE	Jessica Hardwick
ARTHUR	James Edwyn

Director	Stewart Laing
Technical Director	Nick Millar
Cinematographer	Anna Chaney
Lighting Designer	Mike Brookes
Sound Designers	Harry Wilson and Julian Corrie
Choreographer	Ian Spink
Fight Director	Emma Clare Brightlyn
Stage Manager	Avalon Hernandez
Associate Director	Lou Prendergast
Live Producer	Erin Maguire

Untitled Projects are

Artistic Director	Stewart Laing
Executive Producer	Louise Irwin
Board of Directors	Christine Hamilton, David Freer, Carl Lavery, Isobel Lockhart and Fleur Darkin

www.untitledprojects.co.uk

——Projects

ABOUT UNTITLED PROJECTS

Untitled Projects is a Glasgow-based theatre company formed in 1998 by Stewart Laing. Untitled Projects makes ambitious and adventurous theatre on a large scale. We continually re-imagine what theatre can be: blending landscape, biography, novel, video, lecture, documentary, installation, interview, fashion, music, science and playwriting.

Recent Untitled projects include *Paul Bright's Confessions of a Justified Sinner* (National Theatre of Scotland, Tramway and Summerhall); and *The Salon Project* (Traverse, Citizens Theatre and SPILL Festival at the Barbican). Other projects include *Cain's Book* by Alexander Trocchi; *An Argument About Sex* by Pamela Carter, a response to Marivaux's *La Dispute*; and the original production of *Slope* in 2006.

In the 2006 production of *Slope*, the set design preceded the commissioning of the play. The set was a fully functioning Victorian bathroom, with the traditionally 'missing' fourth wall reinstated and the audience watching the action from above, through the 'ceiling'. Access to this viewing position was by way of a sixty-metre sloped floor, after which the play was named. In 2014 we have a new performance space and a new version of the play.

BIOGRAPHIES

Owen Whitelaw trained at the Royal Scottish Academy of Music and Drama. Theatre work includes *Unfaithful* (Traverse); *In Time of Strife* (National Theatre of Scotland); *Paul Bright's Confessions of a Justified Sinner* (Untitled Projects and National Theatre of Scotland); *The Life of Stuff* (Theatre503); *Sleeping Beauty* (Citizens Theatre); *Wonderland* (Vanishing Point); *King Lear* (Citizens Theatre) *and Knives In Hens* (National Theatre of Scotland). On film Owen has appeared in *Dying Light* (RIG Arts); *Score* (Independent); *7/11 In Repeat* (Raging Goose Productions) and *What Would Ridley Do* (Digital Guerillas).

Jessica Hardwick graduated in 2013 from The Royal Conservatoire of Scotland. Previous theatre credits include: *Three Sisters* (Tron Theatre/Kings Theatre Edinburgh); *The Fair Intellectual Club* (Assembly Rooms, Edinburgh Festival Fringe); *Miss Julie* (Citizens Theatre); *Crime and Punishment* (Citizens Theatre/Liverpool Playhouse/Royal Lyceum Edinburgh); *The Possibilities* (Tron Theatre/King's Head Theatre/National Theatre Warsaw); *The Antipodes* (Sam Wanamaker Festival, Shakespeare's Globe). Radio work includes *The Pillow Book* (Series 7, BBC Radio 4). Jessica was the winner on the inaugural Billy Award for Best Newcomer at the Critics Awards for Theatre in Scotland 2014.

James Edwyn graduated from Goldsmiths, University of London in 2014 and *Slope* is his professional debut. Previous theatre credits include: *Romeo and Juliet* (The Cockpit Theatre); *Pope Joan, Ghost Office* (National Youth Theatre); *Oliver* (New Vic Theatre) and a rehearsed reading of *The Grandfathers* (National Theatre).

Pamela Carter has written several Untitled projects including *An Argument About Sex* and *Paul Bright's Confessions of a Justified Sinner*. Other plays include: *Almost Near* (Dresden Staatsshauspiel, Germany; Finborough Theatre, London); *Skåne* (Hampstead Theatre, London; Theater Ulm, Germany; winner of the New Writing Commission at the Berliner Festspiele Stückemarkt, 2012); *What We Know* (Traverse Theatre, Edinburgh; Teatro Circulo, New York). She also works regularly with Swedish conceptual artists Goldin+Senneby (*The Nordenskiöld Model*) and Vanishing Point Theatre Co (including *Interiors* and *Tomorrow*).

Stewart Laing is Artistic Director of Untitled Projects. Directing work elsewhere includes *The Maids* at the Citizens Theatre in Glasgow, *Les Parents Terribles* for Dundee Rep, and *Home: Stornoway* for the National Theatre of Scotland. He has also designed and directed opera in Scotland, elsewhere in the UK and internationally. He designed Richard Jones' production of *Peter Grimes* at La Scala, Milan in 2012. Stewart won a Tony Award in 1998 for his design work on the musical *Titanic*.

Nick Millar is technical manger for Untitled Projects and an artist working, mostly but not exclusively, with his partner Minty Donald. Nick has worked with Untitled since its conception and has a particular interest in the company's use of performance space and their experimental approach to performance conventions. His practice as an artist is multi-disciplinary and generally context-specific, focusing on the interrelations between human and non-human stuff.

Mike Brookes is an award-winning artist, director and designer, whose work has always bridged media. He co-founded the performance collective Pearson/Brookes with Mike Pearson in 1997, most recently co-creating their acclaimed *Coriolan/us* for National Theatre Wales and the RSC. He is currently developing a long- term collaborative practice with Spanish artist Rosa Casado and in 2007 he was appointed Creative Research Fellow within Aberystwyth University.

Anna Chaney is a Scottish artist and filmmaker. Anna graduated from the Royal Conservatoire of Scotland with an Honours degree in Filmmaking. She works commercially as a filmmaker; her artistic practice incorporates film as part of site-specific installation and live performance. Anna has previously collaborated with Fish and Game on their 5 star reviewed 'Alma Mater' projects. These projects have toured internationally since their creation and debut at Charles Rennie Mackintosh's Scotland Street Museum. She worked on Untitled Projects' *The Salon Project* and *Paul Bright's Confessions of Justified Sinner*.

slope

pamela carter

for stewart laing

Characters

MATHILDE VERLAINE
PAUL VERLAINE
ARTHUR RIMBAUD

their ages in act one are seventeen, twenty-seven and eighteen respectively.

Space

a black-box studio theatre.

there are two exits/entrances.

chairs for the audience are placed against all four walls of the studio facing inwards.

there may or may not be pieces of furniture around the edges of the space between the chairs. there may or may not be a bath, or chairs for the actors, for instance.

Punctuation

it comes and goes.

/ – indicates where the next character begins speaking.

… – indicates where a sentence is either abandoned or speech fails.

History

this play mixes fiction with 'historical record'.

Acknowledgments

i'd like to thank the following for their contributions in shaping this play: the cast of the first production, robin laing, kate stannard and sam swainsbury; the cast of this new production, james edwyn, jessica hardwick, and owen whitelaw; agnès jaulent and chris greenwood, my french-language consultants; and stewart laing, whose idea this first was, and whose vision is written deep into the text.

p.c.

This text went to press before the end of rehearsals and so may differ slightly from the play as performed.

Paris

september 1871.

the apartment of MATHILDE'*s parents, mr and mrs de mauté.*

PAUL *and* MATHILDE *moved there for safety at the fall of the paris commune a few months earlier.*

I

the hallway.

PAUL *makes to leave, stops and waits. he turns.*

PAUL	your face. mathilde.
	she comes.
MATHILDE	what is it?
PAUL	your face.
MATHILDE	george is just asleep.
PAUL	let me see.
	she steps towards him.
	it'll be here when i get back?
MATHILDE	of course.
PAUL	promise.
MATHILDE	silly. where else would i be?
PAUL	i need your fairy moon face to light the way.

MATHILDE   i know. the train.
            you should go.

PAUL   where am i going?

MATHILDE   east station.

PAUL   you see.

            he kisses her on the forehead.

MATHILDE   go on paul.

PAUL   i'm going.

            he goes to the door. stops.

            mouse?

MATHILDE   yes.

PAUL   you do love me?

MATHILDE   yes.

PAUL   only you can make me happy.

MATHILDE   and you me.

PAUL   i'm a poet only if you love me.

MATHILDE   and you're such a great poet and your fairy
            loves you so all will be well paul look at the
            time.
            you'll miss the train arriving.
            and then what will happen to our guest?

PAUL   i'm going to meet a genius.

MATHILDE   so you better not be late.

PAUL   what kind of man writes like that.

MATHILDE   you should go and find out.

PAUL   what a responsibility for you mouse.

MATHILDE   it's very exciting. to have two poets to look
            after.

PAUL   look at the time. jesus.
              rimbaud.

              he leaves.

II

MATHILDE *and* ARTHUR *sit in the parlour.* ARTHUR *eats a sandwich greedily.*

MATHILDE *tries not to watch.*

MATHILDE   some sudden business, i'm sure.
              some unavoidable business.
              he can't be long now.
              i hope you won't think ill of us mr rimbaud.

              this is by far the best time to visit paris.
              so much nicer now it's cooler.
              so different to... charleville?

              ARTHUR *grunts assent.*

              charleville.
              i imagine. i've never been.
              we were just in fampoux. with family.
              that's where daddy is now.
              this is daddy's apartment.
              but he's away at the moment.

ARTHUR   (*with mouth full*) fam-poux.

MATHILDE   yes.
              my husband.
              he speaks so very highly of your work.
              your letters to him.
              he's a very fine poet, you think so, don't you.

              in my dreams i'd never thought i'd marry a
              poet.

it's quite a responsibility.
a full-time job.
to keep such a delicate flame alight.
in these dark times.
we had our own apartment before the
commune.
you'd have been very comfortable there,
stayed as long as you liked. i furnished it
myself.
but paul thinks we're safer here.
he's worried he'll be arrested.
refuses to go back to his government job
because he'll be arrested for his part in the
commune.
daddy says he's exaggerating the matter,
says paul didn't do anything really and
everyone knows that.
and it's true he didn't do anything bad at all
but paul's convinced.

and it's so difficult to write when you're
worried about money all the time.
i think.
but he starts a new job tomorrow. daddy
found it for him he has connections.
so everything will be back to normal.

where has he got to?
not thrown in prison. (*laughs at her joke*)

do you intend to stay long, mr rimbaud?
in paris?

ARTHUR   i wrote a new poem.

MATHILDE   oh.

ARTHUR   it's called 'a drunken boat'.

MATHILDE   paul wrote a poem about a boat.

ARTHUR   about pleasure.

MATHILDE	'on a boat'. i meant he wrote a poem called 'on a boat'. that's a metaphor. of course it is.
ARTHUR	yeah?
MATHILDE	i believe so.
ARTHUR	my boat's drunk.
MATHILDE	metaphorically speaking.
	silence.
	perhaps you'd like some cake?
	a door slams.
	this must be him.
(PAUL	carrot.)
MATHILDE	excuse me please. i won't be a moment.
	PAUL *enters.*
	she turns.
	paul / …
PAUL	you're still here.
MATHILDE	where have you been?
PAUL	at the bloody station. north bloody station. / bloody hours wandering…
MATHILDE	shhh. it was east station. i said east.
PAUL	you said north.
MATHILDE	i said east.
PAUL	didn't.
MATHILDE	i did oh it doesn't matter. paul, he's here. mr rimbaud.
PAUL	he's here. how the fuck / did he get here?
MATHILDE	sshhh. i don't know. paul / you haven't…

PAUL   so where is he?

MATHILDE   you've been drinking.

PAUL   no.

MATHILDE   please don't let mummy see.

PAUL   jesus you didn't leave him with her.

MATHILDE   no. he's too dirty.
              i put him in the parlour.
              he doesn't have any luggage.
              paul you're drunk.

PAUL   rimbaud.

MATHILDE   no, wait…

              PAUL *enters the parlour to meet* ARTHUR.

              MATHILDE *follows quickly.*

              here he is.
              here you are.
              paul?
              silly. he went to the wrong station. i said east.
              but look, mr rimbaud found his own way here
              and we've had time to get acquainted.
              paul, why don't you sit down. you're tired.

              PAUL *is swaying.*

              he's been on his feet all this time. looking for
              you.
              sit down paul. you should rest.
              and i can show mr rimbaud to his room.
              let me show you to your room.
              you'd like to rest too, i'm sure.
              freshen up perhaps.
              bathe.
              and then you'll be able to talk sensibly.

              ARTHUR *stands.*

PAUL   how old?

ARTHUR	eighteen.
PAUL	no.
ARTHUR	was only seventeen last year. i call that progress.
PAUL	my god.
	ARTHUR *offers his hand, they shake.*
ARTHUR	arthur.
PAUL	ah.
ARTHUR	rrrrr.
PAUL	th.
ARTHUR	mr verlaine, i'm honoured. really i am.
PAUL	call me paul.
ARTHUR	i will.
PAUL	you met… (*points*)
ARTHUR	the wife.
PAUL	my keeper.
ARTHUR	of the straight and narrow.
PAUL	keeper of the light, arthur.
ARTHUR	mrs verlaine's been telling me about metaphor.
PAUL	no less.
MATHILDE	the room. his room paul.
PAUL	yes. we must have you installed.
	he moves, sways.
	if you'd be so kind, mathilde.
	he sits.

MATHILDE   if you'd like to follow me mr rimbaud.

PAUL   we must do as she says.
arthur.

MATHILDE *opens the door for* ARTHUR
and then follows him out.

PAUL *sits staring after them. he falls asleep.*

III

the bathroom.

PAUL   god. oh god.

ARTHUR *appears at the doorway.*

give me strength.

ARTHUR   for cowards and cretins.

PAUL   what?

ARTHUR   i said 'for cowards and cretins'.

PAUL   bathing or clerking?

ARTHUR   god.

PAUL   aah.

ARTHUR   don't you reckon?

PAUL   i'm a natural optimist.

ARTHUR   don't know what clerking is for.

PAUL   lucky you.

ARTHUR   bathing's no concern to me.

PAUL   but of great concern to my wife.

ARTHUR   i don't like water.

PAUL	as she has remarked.
ARTHUR	i like dirt.
PAUL	–
ARTHUR	the smell of shit.
	ARTHUR *enters and closes the door.*
PAUL	dear arthur, you're mathilde's worst nightmare taken human form. she is a respectable woman.
ARTHUR	dirt. this is how it is. this is real life.
PAUL	she is a romantic.
	ARTHUR *picks up some soap, sniffs it and throws it away.*
ARTHUR	does she smell like that?
PAUL	can't rightly remember.
ARTHUR	oh poor paul.
PAUL	poor paul indeed.
ARTHUR	it's our job to experience life, isn't it?
PAUL	sometimes.
ARTHUR	all of it, all the time.
PAUL	but it's painful arthur.
ARTHUR	it's our job to suffer. we're artists.
PAUL	i suffer. don't have any worries there.
ARTHUR	so the cowards and cretins will know the truth.
PAUL	what are you capable of. you're barely a man. and no man in paris, no artist i know sees the world like you.
ARTHUR	because what i see hasn't happened yet.

PAUL	you're here from the future to tell us about it.
ARTHUR	we are here to make it happen.
PAUL	you. you are.
ARTHUR	you and me. only we can know the truth.
PAUL	but the truth is so very dark.
ARTHUR	we got a job to do. we got art to save. the world to save.
PAUL	i'm a poet not a priest. it's hard enough trying to save myself.
ARTHUR	we are the priests, paul. not those fat kiddy-fiddlers in frocks. we know the truth and it's shitty and brutal. and it's our job to tell people what's really going on. and you're the high priest. and i'm here so you can make me your neophyte. and together, we'll teach those know-nothing fuckwits what life is, what art is.

MATHILDE *knocks on the door.*

(MATHILDE	paul. i've your shirt ready.)
PAUL	christ.
ARTHUR	you're the only poet alive gives me a hard-on.
PAUL	shut up.
(MATHILDE	paul? paul?)

he splashes water.

PAUL	washing. washing.
ARTHUR	(*whispers*) a hard-on, i tell you.
(MATHILDE	i'll put it on our bed.)

PAUL   she wants me dead. and that tight-bastard
                father of hers. they may as well hand me to
                the police themselves.

ARTHUR   so skip the office.

PAUL   you think i do this out of choice?
                i'm entirely at their mercy.

ARTHUR   i'll come with you then.
                assist you in your duties. your clerky duties.

PAUL   you could be my ammanuensis.

ARTHUR   you'll wonder how you ever did without me.

PAUL   –

ARTHUR   and then seeing as we're out.
                maybe there are some sights you'd like to
                show me. places where the great poets of
                paris gather and great words are spoken.

PAUL   i know a café or two.

ARTHUR   we could have a drink. if you like.

PAUL   why not.

ARTHUR   live a little.

PAUL   yes.

ARTHUR   get fucked up.

PAUL   i'd like to make a toast, arthur.

ARTHUR   to our new church.

PAUL   but all we have is water.
                still a church needs ceremony.
                come here. closer. my little pagan poet.

                he puts a hand round the back of ARTHUR's
                neck.

                that's it. i baptise / you…

ARTHUR   i'm not going / in there.

                PAUL *grabs* ARTHUR *and pulls him to the*
                bath.

PAUL   in the name of art, truth, i baptise you. and
                you shall be called...

ARTHUR   you'll be sorry...

PAUL   ...'my evil genius'.

                PAUL *ducks* ARTHUR*'s head into the water.*

                MATHILDE *knocks on the door.*

(MATHILDE   paul. what are you doing?)

PAUL   cleansing my sins.

                ARTHUR *struggles just a little and gasps for*
                air laughing and spluttering.

(MATHILDE   don't make a mess.)

ARTHUR   fucking hell.

                ARTHUR *grabs* PAUL *and pushes his head*
                under.

(MATHILDE   are you well paul?)

ARTHUR   (*mimicking* MATHILDE) are you well paul?

                PAUL *comes up for air spluttering.*

(MATHILDE   paul?)

PAUL   yes. fine. fine.
                you cunt.

                PAUL *grabs* ARTHUR *by the neck.*

(MATHILDE   don't be long.)

ARTHUR   you and me.

PAUL   you're going to break my heart arthur. aren't
                you.

ARTHUR   your appointment.

                PAUL *lets go of* ARTHUR.

PAUL   we should get a move on.

                ARTHUR *goes for the door.*

                what the fuck are you doing? stop. jesus.
                you can't just walk out like that.

ARTHUR   why?

PAUL   she'll see you.

ARTHUR   and?

PAUL   wait here.
                i have to look like i've washed.
                do i look like i've washed?
                oh this is unbearable. life is unbearable.
                stay here.
                don't move.
                i'll call you when it's clear.

                PAUL *leaves carefully closing the door
                behind him.*

ARTHUR   A... E... I... O... U...

                A black, E white, I red... ready or not ...

                ARTHUR *opens the door and exits.*

IV

MATHILDE *enters the bedroom and tries to close the door behind her.*

(PAUL	don't you walk away from me.)
	PAUL *throws the door open.*
MATHILDE	i don't know / why you're…
PAUL	you say that again.
MATHILDE	don't shout please, mummy / will…
	PAUL *slams the door shut behind him.*
	george is sleeping i don't know what you want me to say.
PAUL	i want you to repeat what you just said to me.
MATHILDE	i didn't say anything. really i don't know why you're so upset.
PAUL	you think i imagined this this… look.
	he holds out his shaking hands to her.
MATHILDE	that's alcohol.
PAUL	i have feelings.
MATHILDE	george needs me.
PAUL	fuck george. what did you call arthur?
MATHILDE	i only said what walter said. 'miss rimbaud.' he called arthur 'miss rimbaud'. / that's all…
PAUL	fucking hell.
MATHILDE	they'll hear. mummy / and…
PAUL	i don't give a shit.
MATHILDE	paul, please.
PAUL	is that what they're saying?

MATHILDE	don't shout.
PAUL	then answer me. is that what they're saying?
MATHILDE	what?
PAUL	that i'm a faggot.
MATHILDE	i don't know what you're talking about.
PAUL	you stupid cow.

he snatches the book out of her hand – it's
madame bovary *by gustave flaubert – and*
throws it on the floor.

this doesn't fool anyone, you know.
a faggot. a queer.
jesus.
a homosexual.

MATHILDE	a what?
PAUL	a homosexual.
MATHILDE	–
PAUL	oh god.
MATHILDE	oh the / saints…
PAUL	that's it. that's what they're saying. boys?
MATHILDE	oh.
PAUL	that's what your poisonous moron of a brother is saying about me.
MATHILDE	why…
PAUL	and his fucking halfwit friends.
MATHILDE	why would walter say something as awful as that.
PAUL	those cunts. they call themselves artists.
MATHILDE	i misheard him.

PAUL	they're trying to ruin me. if the police hear… if the police find out. they'll arrest me. i'll go to court. i'll go to prison.
MATHILDE	but it's a mistake.
PAUL	no one will speak to me ever again.
MATHILDE	but it's not true. it can't be true.
PAUL	and you. you'll be ruined too.
MATHILDE	i haven't done anything.
PAUL	oh my god. you'll divorce me. you'll divorce me, won't you? that bastard father of yours will divorce me.
MATHILDE	paul / no…
PAUL	it's him spreading these lies. that fucker'd stoop to anything to get rid of me. you can't divorce me mathilde. it's not allowed.
MATHILDE	i know.
PAUL	you can't leave me. it's a sin.
MATHILDE	daddy can't hear this when he gets back.
PAUL	i'd never be able to write again. i'd die without you. please mathilde. i'm begging you. don't leave me.
MATHILDE	i won't leave you paul i can't. we're married. i'm only seventeen.
PAUL	what a mess. a foggy mess. and i'm all alone.

MATHILDE   but it's not. you're not.
             what about me. what about george.

PAUL   i don't know how much more of this i can
             take.

MATHILDE   paul it'll be alright. paul listen.

PAUL   i'm fucked.

MATHILDE   we can be happy again. like we were in the
             beginning.
             everything will be fine.

PAUL   how? how is it? go on, you tell me.

MATHILDE   because it's not true.
             and those people can't say those things can
             they if it's not true.
             you can't be arrested and sent to prison for
             something you haven't done.

PAUL   what?

MATHILDE   because you're not...

PAUL   what?

MATHILDE   it's him.

PAUL   what are you talking about?

MATHILDE   giving people the wrong impression.
             he's the one causing all the trouble. we were
             getting along just fine before he turned up.
             so if you just tell him to go.

PAUL   –

MATHILDE   you'll prove it's not true.

PAUL   i don't need to prove anything.

MATHILDE   yes, i know that paul. but / they...

PAUL   no buts. i don't need to prove anything.
             i am innocent.

MATHILDE   i know. but i think that if you ask mr rimbaud
            to leave then you'll show to everyone else
            there's nothing… nothing. and then when
            daddy gets home rimbaud will be gone and he
            won't know anything at all and it will be like
            rimbaud was never here.
            paul?

PAUL   you think it's true.
            you think i'm fucking arthur.

MATHILDE   no.

PAUL   it's you.

MATHILDE   –

PAUL   it's you. telling these lies so he'll have to
            leave.
            you're jealous. and you hate him. you hate
            dear arthur.

MATHILDE   no he hates me.

PAUL   you want to get rid of him because he makes
            me happy. you hate me.

MATHILDE   no.

PAUL   cruel pitiless.

MATHILDE   no it's him. he is.

PAUL   he's a genius.

MATHILDE   no he's not.

PAUL   he is great.

MATHILDE   no he's not. he's bad. i've seen the way he
            looks at me.
            he laughs at me. he snarls at me. he's dirty.
            the way he eats. he's like a dog.
            a nasty mangy dog.

PAUL   it's you.

MATHILDE   it's him.
            he doesn't do anything. he's disgusting. and
            he smells.
            he has lice paul. he has lice.

PAUL   you bitch.

MATHILDE   don't call me that.

PAUL   you're my wife. i can call you anything / i
            like. bitch.
            lying bitch.

MATHILDE   i've done nothing wrong.
            it's not fair. it wasn't meant to be like this.
            you said you loved me.
            i only married you because you said you
            loved me.
            you said you'd look after me.

PAUL   don't / start that.

MATHILDE   and you wrote poems for me but you don't
            mean any of it.

PAUL   every word every / word is…

MATHILDE   you don't love me. you don't even like me.

PAUL   –

MATHILDE   you're a drunk.

PAUL   i'm a poet.

MATHILDE   no one likes your poetry.
            only he does. ratboy. only him.
            you used to say beautiful things to me.
            and now we have to live here. and we've got
            no money.
            and you're nasty to me.
            i don't know why this is happening.
            you're my husband.

PAUL   i'll fucking show / you…

he pushes her against the wall.

MATHILDE   no…

PAUL   say you're sorry, girl.

MATHILDE   don't hit me.

PAUL   then say it.

MATHILDE   let me go.

PAUL   apologise for saying those terrible things about me.

MATHILDE   sorry.

PAUL   and arthur. say it.

MATHILDE   sorry.

PAUL   it's not right. you're my wife.

MATHILDE   i said i'm sorry. i'm sorry.

he lets go of her.

PAUL   thank you.

he straightens his clothes.

that's all i wanted to hear.

he goes to the door.

i'm going out for a while now. i won't be back for dinner.

he leaves.

MATHILDE *is crying.*

ARTHUR *appears at the doorway.*

ARTHUR   up up. rise up, woman.
free yourself.
you could be a poet too.

MATHILDE   what do you want?

ARTHUR   everything.

ARTHUR steps into the room and aside for MATHILDE.

hold up…

he picks up MATHILDE's book from the floor and holds it out to her.

it doesn't end well, you know.

as she approaches he feints a jab at her with the book, she yelps, snatches it and runs out.

V

a bedroom.

ARTHUR is preparing a glass of absinthe: the spoon, burning the sugar, dripping water in so it turns white.

PAUL enters.

PAUL   for christ's sake, arthur.
                you can't do that here. at least close the door.

                he closes the door.

                she's so vigilant.
                arthur.

ARTHUR   matches.

                PAUL hands him a box of matches.

PAUL   i need to say something.

ARTHUR   –

PAUL   we can't go on like this.
                arthur. we can't go on like this.

                ARTHUR nods in agreement.

this, for instance. you know i can't have this
sort of thing in the apartment. it's not my
apartment.

ARTHUR *offers* PAUL *the glass of absinthe.*

if it were my apartment...

he takes the glass.

but it's not. they're not my rules.
it's a matter of respect.

he gives the glass back to ARTHUR.

not absinthe, not today.

ARTHUR   last night.

PAUL   last night. exactly.

ARTHUR   fucking civil servants.

PAUL   you see. that's what i'm talking about arthur.

ARTHUR   you're either an artist or an office worker. not
            both.

PAUL   they are artists and they deserve respect. some
            of them.

ARTHUR   big vocabularies, tiny lives.

PAUL   no. did you hear charles? did you hear what
            he said?

ARTHUR   yeah. and?

PAUL   mars. he's going to communicate with, with,
            what did he call them.

ARTHUR   extra-terrestrial beings.

PAUL   extra-beings. yes. it's extra-ordinary. imagine
            arthur.
            all it takes is a big mirror over paris and we
            can shine messages to mars.

ARTHUR	charles is a cunt.
PAUL	but he's a clever cunt and…

ARTHUR *is preparing himself an absinthe*.

arthur, really… please stop that.

ARTHUR	they're all cunts. with their stupid fucking rules. art needs chaos. fuck rules.
PAUL	but you can't go around stabbing people.
ARTHUR	i was provoked.
PAUL	no one interrupts when someone is giving their poem. shouting 'shit' after every line.
ARTHUR	someone had to do something.
PAUL	you don't think how your behaviour reflects on me, arthur. you don't think about me.
ARTHUR	all that describing and no action.
PAUL	that may well be.
ARTHUR	it was shit.
PAUL	you do know theo's been reprinted.
ARTHUR	he's shit. they're all shit. all of them. we're going to write stuff that'll blow their tight arses wide open, paul. and that fucker theodore is going to kiss your shitty shoes soon. he'll be parting his cheeks in supplication. on his knees begging to suck your cock. and mine.
PAUL	your lovely cock.
ARTHUR	we haven't even started yet, paul. you haven't even started yet. we're going to change the world.

PAUL   not now…

ARTHUR   not sitting round here, rhyming dirty ditties
                with those pricks you won't.

PAUL   we're a movement.

ARTHUR   thirty. over fucking thirty and look at them.
                should be ashamed of themselves, calling
                themselves poets.
                they should be dead. if i'm not dead by the
                time i'm thirty i've fucked up.

PAUL   i'm twenty-seven.

ARTHUR   so you've got three years left to be great in
                paul.

PAUL   i don't want to die.

ARTHUR   here.

                he offers PAUL *the absinthe again.*

                PAUL *looks at the glass but doesn't take it.*

PAUL   i can't.

ARTHUR   i'm only here because of you.

PAUL   no.
                arthur, what i'm trying to say
                is that we need to be a little more
                circumspect.
                people are talking about us.
                telling lies.

ARTHUR   and you give a shit?

PAUL   mathilde's father, he gives a shit.
                he has business interests.

ARTHUR   fuck mr mauté.

PAUL   yes so this is the crux of the matter, arthur.
                fuck mr mauté. fuck mr mauté will be home
                this evening and i want i need everything to

	look normal when he does so and as you refuse to make yourself presentable or make any concession to maintaining the status quo then mathilde thinks it's better if you leave before he returns.
ARTHUR	'mathilde thinks'?
PAUL	yes.
ARTHUR	you're a fucking coward, paul.
PAUL	i'm not a fucking coward. i'm a responsible fucking adult. nothing you'd know anything about. you must go today. today. or mathilde will tell her father about the rumours and we'll both end up in jail.
ARTHUR	where will i go?
PAUL	charles. he's still speaking to you. you can stay with him.
ARTHUR	i haven't got any money.
PAUL	mathilde said she'd give you some if you go.
ARTHUR	–
PAUL	arthur. artie. listen to me. i've got it all worked out. you go stay with charles. domestic harmony is restored. i carry on pretending to go to work. we meet in cafés. we continue our project away from mathilde and her fucking father. art will be saved and history will glorify us.
ARTHUR	it's not enough.
PAUL	how can that not be enough?
ARTHUR	have a drink with me.

PAUL	i can't. you know what it does to me.
ARTHUR	fuck it. fuck it paul. let's get out of here.
PAUL	are you listening arthur. my father-in-law returns today. i have to be here.
ARTHUR	paris. let's get out of paris.
PAUL	what?
ARTHUR	paris is fucking over, man. london's where it's at. that's where we should be.
PAUL	what are you talking about?
ARTHUR	london. you and me. we can be together in london. let's go to london.
PAUL	and do what?
ARTHUR	write. drink. fuck.
PAUL	–
ARTHUR	we can do whatever we want.
PAUL	you'd have me destroy everything.
ARTHUR	that's the project. get with the project.
PAUL	but you don't know how black it gets.
ARTHUR	yes i do. here.
	he offers PAUL *the glass of absinthe again.*
PAUL	there's no poetry in darkness like that.
ARTHUR	there is. you haven't found it yet that's all. have a drink.
PAUL	no.
ARTHUR	one won't hurt.
	PAUL *grabs* ARTHUR *by the neck.*

PAUL   you fucking incubus.

ARTHUR   one little drink, paul. have one with me and
                then i'll go. promise. i'll go and you can have
                a quiet night with the wife and the in-laws
                and fuck mr mauté'll never know i was here.
                one for the road. please.

                PAUL *lets go of* ARTHUR.

PAUL   this is impossible.

                ARTHUR *offers* PAUL *the glass and he
                takes it*.

ARTHUR   not for the likes of you and me.

                they drink.

VI

the parlour.

MATHILDE *is holding baby george*.

PAUL   are you not hot, mouse?

MATHILDE   not at all. i'm just right.

PAUL   but it's so hot.
                and airless.

MATHILDE   why don't you open the window.

                he goes to the window.

PAUL   not if you're just right.

MATHILDE   i don't mind.

PAUL   no no.

                silence.

	my chest. it's like a beast sitting on my chest. its face there stealing my breath.
MATHILDE	you'll feel better soon.
PAUL	i can't breathe.
MATHILDE	open the window then.
PAUL	he won't catch a chill?
MATHILDE	it's a mild evening.
PAUL	poor mite.
MATHILDE	he's well wrapped.
	silence.
PAUL	he's not damaged.
MATHILDE	he's fine now.
PAUL	i can't remember a thing.
MATHILDE	you were drunk.
PAUL	monstrous. in drink.
MATHILDE	yes.
PAUL	but harmless sober.
MATHILDE	yes paul.
PAUL	will he forgive me?
MATHILDE	i'm sure. he's only a baby. you love your daddy, don't you george. i'm sure i don't remember anything before i was two even three. i can remember / playing in the garden and i had ribbons…
PAUL	but the way he looks at me.
MATHILDE	he'll forget. he's forgotten already.
	silence.

PAUL   i'm so very hot.
                burning.

MATHILDE   open the window.

                *he opens the window, breathes deeply,
                coughs.*

PAUL   better. that's better.
                but george...

MATHILDE   he's fine.

PAUL   i don't want him to hate me.

MATHILDE   he won't. as long as it doesn't happen again.

                he closes the window.

PAUL   i'd never forgive myself if i made him ill.

MATHILDE   i know.

PAUL   oh i need to breathe.

MATHILDE   sunday, paul.
                pasdeloup's orchestra will play on the
                bandstand this sunday.
                we could walk out and see the concert
                together.
                mummy and daddy... your mother too.
                you can go out on sunday.
                that'll be fresh air enough.
                and music.
                music always makes you feel better.
                sunday you can go out.
                and meantime, why not leave the window
                open.

                PAUL *sits down again.*

London

1872–3.

squalid lodgings in camden.

I

ARTHUR *enters.*

ARTHUR   …telling you. this is where it's gonna happen.
this city.

a boot flies past him.

PAUL   i can't believe you made me walk that far.
owww.

PAUL enters trying to pull the other boot off.

ARTHUR   it's a great monster machine.
fucking itself and eating itself.
and shitting itself out.
so many people starving and diseased. i
swear…

PAUL throws the boot and hits ARTHUR.

cunt.
never seen deformities like it.

PAUL   come here.

ARTHUR   what misery.
what noise. cacophonous. shouting fighting
fucking chaos.
and the stench. everyone stinks.

PAUL *is undoing* ARTHUR*'s trousers.*

PAUL	i thought you liked that.
ARTHUR	love it. it's perfect. it's babylon-don. perfect. i thought poor pauline was tired. that boy in the 'pissoir' not enough for you?
PAUL	a 'canapé'.
ARTHUR	i could've saved you the money.
PAUL	you said it's our duty to experience. everything. and he was so cheap. besides. we're on holiday.
ARTHUR	we're not on fucking holiday. we're here to work.
PAUL	this is working. isn't it?
ARTHUR	maybe.
PAUL	this is the project.
ARTHUR	part of it.
PAUL	where's the oil?
ARTHUR	it's time to write.

PAUL *empties the remains of a bottle of oil into his hands, rubbing it into* ARTHUR*'s arse and his own cock.*

PAUL   let me penetrate you.
i won't be long.

they fuck.

this is working artie.
your lovely arsehole. your dirty 'o' 'o' …

ARTHUR   this is the place.
i was right. wasn't i right?

deranged.
twisted.

PAUL   the beginning and the end.
i love you artie.
you won't ever leave me, will you?
will you?

ARTHUR   you're so sentimental.

PAUL   everything's here. in the dark. in the shit.

ARTHUR   hang on...

he shifts position.

PAUL   okay?

ARTHUR   yeah.

PAUL   everything. and nothing. deep inside. like
home. like i'm home. i'm home i'm home i'm
oh.

PAUL *comes.*

ARTHUR   happy now?

PAUL   sad now.
hold me, artie. hold me.

ARTHUR   in a minute.

ARTHUR *is taking care of himself.*

london.
this is as new as it gets.
you can buy anything sell anything in this
city.
this is what modern means.
and we're here.
and this is it.
this is it.
we're here.

ARTHUR *comes.*

PAUL   i like watching you come. your expression.
                   it's like you pass into another world and back.
                   it's like you're back from the dead.

ARTHUR   give me that.

                   PAUL *passes a shirt to him and* ARTHUR
                   wipes his cock and hands with it.

                   the smoke and the steam. tunnels gouged out
                   of the ground.

PAUL   that's mine. it was almost clean.

                   ARTHUR *throws it back at* PAUL.

ARTHUR   the violence. it's the end of the classical
                   world.
                   it's the end of metre and rhyme.
                   it has to be.

PAUL   they're brutes. the anglo-saxons.
                   brutish.

ARTHUR   infernal.

PAUL   all black and burnt.
                   like the food.
                   although the fruit-and-meat thingy.
                   that thingy gave us.

ARTHUR   vermersch.

PAUL   yes vermersch. that he gave us.
                   goose. with apples.
                   superb.
                   who would've thought it.

                   and the uniforms.
                   those lovely young men in red uniforms.
                   at thingy. the palace of buckingham.

                   and the plumbing. much better than home.
                   marvellous.
                   really marvellous.

ARTHUR *is writing*.

but they're all so thin. and poor.
don't you think?
and me.
i'm so thin.
artie. look at me.
i'm very thin.
and poor.

and the place is riddled with spies.
you know this don't you? you are aware of
this?
crawling with them.
consorting with lissagaray and andrieu and
vermersch.
they're wanted men. fugitives.
we're being watched i can feel it. we'll be
reported back to paris.
verlaine. rimbaud.
communards. terrorists.

ARTHUR   no going back to paris now.

PAUL   no.

ARTHUR   never.

PAUL   this place is disgusting.
            what am i to do.

            ARTHUR *throws a notebook at* PAUL.

            owwww.

ARTHUR   write.

            they both work.

II

they are lying with their arms around each other.

ARTHUR	written that letter yet? hey. have you?
PAUL	no.
ARTHUR	why not?
PAUL	–
ARTHUR	we're running out of money.
PAUL	i know.
ARTHUR	so.
PAUL	–
ARTHUR	we need to eat.
PAUL	–
ARTHUR	and more gin. go on paul.
PAUL	why why must i. humiliate myself.
ARTHUR	you've done it before. bit late for shame now.
PAUL	the situation calls for delicacy. not that i expect you to understand such a concept. why don't you ask your mother?
ARTHUR	because it's your turn.
PAUL	because she's a stingy old witch.
ARTHUR	you said you would.
PAUL	don't nag. i've got a wife.
ARTHUR	not for much longer.
PAUL	screw you. she won't divorce me.

ARTHUR	the law's changing.
PAUL	well she won't leave me then. she's a respectable woman.
ARTHUR	can't think of a more impoverished state than that of a 'respectable woman'. at least with a whore you know what she's fucking you for.

ARTHUR picks up a bottle to finish it off.

PAUL	hey.
ARTHUR	you've had more than me.

PAUL snatches the bottle back.

PAUL	you drink because it's an adventure. i drink because i have to.

he holds the bottle up to his mouth.

ARTHUR	don't.
PAUL	or what?

he drinks. ARTHUR *slaps him and* PAUL *punches back.*

ARTHUR	cunt.
PAUL	fucker.

they slap and punch each other. eventually ARTHUR *bites* PAUL *on the thigh.*

you bit me. that's not fair. you bit me. arthur. that's not fair.

he spits.

ARTHUR	shit.

PAUL *is rolling his trouser leg up.*

PAUL	look. look what you did. most likely i'm infected now. i'll die here.

	and my poor mother will find me.
	the putrid corpse of paul verlaine, poet
	manky.

ARTHUR   manqué.

PAUL   whatever.

ARTHUR   right.
           time to learn something.

PAUL   piss off you animal.

ARTHUR   do you good.
           occupy your mind.

PAUL   don't patronise me you vicious peasant.

ARTHUR   it's the / project.

PAUL   and shut up about the bloody project.
           i don't give a fuck about the project.

ARTHUR   je m'en branle.

PAUL   piss off.

ARTHUR   je – me – en – m'en – branle.
           i – do – not – don't give a fuck. in english.

PAUL   je m'en... what?

ARTHUR   branle.

PAUL   branle.

ARTHUR   se branler.

PAUL   to fuck?

ARTHUR   to wank.

PAUL   very english.

ARTHUR   so. se branler.
           come on. it's regular. you can conjugate it.
           come on.
           he wanks...

PAUL   il se branle.

ARTHUR   she wanks.

PAUL   surely not.

ARTHUR   paul.

PAUL   elle se branle.

ARTHUR   i wank, you wank, we wank, they wank.

PAUL   je me branle.
              tu... think we've reached that stage in our
              relationship... tu te branles...
              nous nous branlons, ils se branlent et cetera et
              cetera et cetera.

ARTHUR   you should take the project more seriously.

PAUL   but i don't wank myself about your project.

ARTHUR   what?

PAUL   je m'en branle.

ARTHUR   i give a fuck.

PAUL   you said 'wank'.

ARTHUR   literally. literally wank.
              but not in sense... not in usage.

PAUL   stupid fucking language. why can't they say
              what they mean.
              there's no clarity.

ARTHUR   i like it.

PAUL   no rules.

ARTHUR   i like it. it's hard and roguish. a bastard
              language.
              the language of bastards and half-breeds and
              fags.

PAUL   i don't know how one is supposed to empty
              one's heart with it.

ARTHUR	cock.
PAUL	what?
ARTHUR	what's the english for 'cock'?
PAUL	la bitte, la pine, la teub, le zob, le cigare, le zizi, la queue, la quequette, membre, phallus…
ARTHUR	very good. arse.
PAUL	le cul.
ARTHUR	arsehole.
PAUL	cul… hule? oh hell.
ARTHUR	you should know this.
PAUL	intimately.
ARTHUR	arsehole.
PAUL	you're terrible to me.
ARTHUR	l'oignon.
PAUL	say what?
ARTHUR	l'oignon.
PAUL	onion? are you serious?
ARTHUR	yes.
PAUL	your holy onion?
ARTHUR	yes. so. i want to stick it up your arsehole.
PAUL	je veux… te… le… carrer dans l'oignon?
ARTHUR	that's it.
PAUL	how quaint.
ARTHUR	cum.

PAUL   jus. now i like the sound of this. jus.

ARTHUR   come on me.

PAUL   jouis sur moi.

ARTHUR   so formal?

PAUL   huh? oh. jouis – moi dessus.

PAUL *has his head on* ARTHUR*'s chest and his hand in* ARTHUR*'s trousers. he's falling asleep.*

ARTHUR   swallow. avaler.

PAUL   swallow.

ARTHUR   'avaler.'

PAUL   yes.

ARTHUR   say it.

PAUL   yes.

ARTHUR   say 'avaler'.

PAUL   avaler.

ARTHUR   i want to swallow your cum.

PAUL   mmm.

ARTHUR   i want to swallow your cum.
                je veux t'avaler le jus.
                paul. paul.

ARTHUR *finds a book to read:* l'ami commun *by charles dickens.*

III

PAUL *stares out of the window. he is cold.*

PAUL   pitter patter.
               pitter patter.
               sad sad.

               even the rain is black.

               this is miserable.

ARTHUR   give me that.

               PAUL *gives him his notebook and watches*
               ARTHUR *as he reads.*

PAUL   you're laughing.

ARTHUR   i'm not.

PAUL   you are. what are you laughing at? tell me.

ARTHUR   nothing.

PAUL   don't say 'nothing'.

               ARTHUR *continues reading.*

               that's my heart you're holding. don't you
               smirk and say 'nothing'.
               spit it out. not like you to spare my feelings.

ARTHUR   the girl.

PAUL   what girl?

ARTHUR   this girl.

PAUL   she's you arthur.

ARTHUR   i know.

PAUL   so.

ARTHUR   –

PAUL   well. 'she' is the expression of an idea, a
               feeling more… many people, when they read

the poems, will understand.
and i favour the sound. 'sshh.' the texture. the
soft tissue.
it's so...

ARTHUR   feminine.

PAUL   you know and that's all that matters. other
                people. they wouldn't understand.

ARTHUR   tough business this truth-telling.

PAUL   they wouldn't understand. all they're
                interested in is who's sticking what to whom.
                if i wrote, well if i put 'he' they'd they'd twist
                my meaning turn it into something dirty.
                profane.

ARTHUR   you'd be arrested you mean.

PAUL   no i don't mean that. this isn't dirt.
                this is pure.

ARTHUR   two little girls? we're two little girls?

PAUL   oh for christ's sake. it's a state of grace arthur.
                a feeling. innocence. do you know what that
                is?
                were you ever innocent?

                pause.

ARTHUR   it's good.

                he throws the notebook back to PAUL –
                gently.

PAUL   show me yours.

ARTHUR   later.

                ARTHUR *closes his notebook and picks up a
                book* – journey to the centre of the earth *by
                jules verne.*

                PAUL *drinks.*

PAUL   i'm bored.

ARTHUR   you haven't finished.

PAUL   i've seen enough of my sickly soul for one day.
                 god.
                 look at this place.
                 look at the stains on these walls.
                 making faces. disappointed faces at me.
                 let's go out.

                 he pulls out a couple of coins from a pocket.

                 le pub.

ARTHUR   later.

PAUL   sightseeing?
                 there must be some heap of cultural
                 significance you haven't dragged me round
                 yet.

ARTHUR   –

PAUL   london tower.

ARTHUR   tower of london.

PAUL   there.

ARTHUR   no.

PAUL   ohh.

                 pause.

                 i wonder what they're saying about us in
                 montmartre.

ARTHUR   –

PAUL   a change of clothes would be nice.
                 and an absinthe.
                 to be in the arms of the green goddess
                 oblivion in her arms.
                 how long has it been?
                 artie?
                 ten months. a year…

ARTHUR	fucking hell.
	he throws his book down.
PAUL	but you'd like an absinthe /...
ARTHUR	you're not going back.
	pause.
PAUL	why don't you read to me?
ARTHUR	read what?
PAUL	i don't know. anything. english if you like.
ARTHUR	–
PAUL	what about whatsisname?
ARTHUR	who?
PAUL	poo. arthur poo.
ARTHUR	poe. edgar allan poe.
PAUL	that's him. read him.
ARTHUR	right.
	ARTHUR *finds a poem.*
	we must entertain poor homesick paul. here's just the one for you. 'à ma mere'... 'to my mother' by edgar allan poe.
PAUL	–
ARTHUR	'à ma mere'. 'Parce que je crois qu'aux cieux dessus, Les anges, se chuchotant, Ne sachent / trouver, parmi...'
PAUL	wait. wait. wait. what was that about les anges? angels. is this a queer poem?
ARTHUR	think he's one of us?
PAUL	them. one of them.

ARTHUR   angels, whispering to each other,
                can't find... parmi... their... burning words
                of love,
                'Un terme si dévot que "Ô mere"'...
                a term as devotional as 'mother.'

PAUL   it's very ugly.

ARTHUR   'Ainsi ai-je longtemps te nommée,
                Toi, qui es beaucoup plus qu'une mère pour
                moi.
                / Et qui remplis le cœur de mon cœur, Là
                Où la Mort t'a installée,
                En lâchant échapper l'esprit
                De ma chère Mathilde.'

PAUL   lumbering like an un-milked cow.
                blah blah blah why is he successful and not
                me.
                moaning about his mother. did you say /
                mathilde?

ARTHUR   shut up and listen. it's not about his mother.

PAUL   well what the fuck's he going on about then?

ARTHUR   shut up and you might find out.
                'Ma mère, ma mère à moi, qui tôt est morte,
                Ne fut que la mère de moi-même; mais Toi,
                Étant mère à celle que j'aimais tant' / ...

PAUL   whose mother? whose arsing mother?

ARTHUR   the in-laws paul.
                it's a poem for the mother of his dear dead
                wife. hey? i chose this poem just for you.
                thought it might put a smile on that pasty
                face. cheers me up no end.
                'M'es plus chère que la mère que j'ai connue
                Par cette infinité que ma chère femme
                / Était plus chère à mon âme que sa propre vie
                d'âme.'

PAUL   you cunt. you vile cunt. that's horrible.

ARTHUR   but you are mother to the one i loved so
          dearly,
          and blah are dearer than the mother i knew
          by how much, paulie?
          by that infinity... which my wife
          was dearer to my soul than i dunno / the life
          of my soul... to its own. itself. is to itself oh
          bollocks.

PAUL   you despicable cunt. don't you say that.
          she's not dead.

ARTHUR   she may as well be.

PAUL   how dare you how dare / you ...

ARTHUR   'how dare you how dare you'
          fucking mathilde and / her ugly baby and her
          stingy bitch of a mother.

PAUL   how dare you invoke her name in this sordid
          shitpit.
          besmirch her precious name.
          you leave her out of this. / she doesn't deserve
          this hell.

ARTHUR   me leave her out of it? you leave her out of it.
          you feeble prick.

PAUL   i've already left her.

ARTHUR   can't get rid of the witch.

PAUL   are you mad? i'm here. alone.

ARTHUR   i warned you about backsliding you stinking
          streak of piss.

PAUL   i don't know what you're talking about.

ARTHUR   you forget about her and paris. you're staying
          right here.
          with me.

PAUL   oh arthur, i'm afraid you are raving.

ARTHUR   i know what you're up to.

PAUL   you are a very sick man.

ARTHUR   give me that letter.

                he goes for the the inside pocket of PAUL*'s
                jacket.*

PAUL   get off me.

ARTHUR   give it here.

PAUL   get off me you fucking madman. i don't have
                a letter. bastard.

                they fight, PAUL *trying to get away from*
                ARTHUR.

                no…

ARTHUR   i'll kill you…

PAUL   help. help me. fuck… owwww…

                ARTHUR *gets the better of* PAUL. *he has
                him on the floor and pulls a letter out of his
                pocket.*

                no. that's mine. don't touch that.

                ARTHUR *has his boot on the back of* PAUL*'s
                neck to keep him down.* ARTHUR *opens the
                letter.*

                it's private.

ARTHUR   nothing's private, pig. i see everything.
                nothing's private in here.

                he reads the letter.

PAUL   it's not for you.

ARTHUR   'my carrot fairy princess, how i have missed
                you, dear heart.
                i can bear your absence no longer and will
                surely die if you won't take me back into the
                bosom of our home.'

the mighty poet verlaine turns his hand to prose for teenage girls.

'take no heed of the malicious and entirely false rumours circulating paris about the innocent relationship with my unruly pupil, the young villain rimbaud...'

PAUL   let me go.

ARTHUR   genius. fucking genius.

'meet me in brussels at the hotel liégeois...' you're not going anywhere you bugger. not to brussels. not to paris. or wherever you think it's safe to meet that cunting carrot bitch.

he rips the letter up and throws it at PAUL.

we haven't finished.

PAUL   look what you've done to me. what more do you want?

ARTHUR   everything. that's the deal.

PAUL   i can't live like this.

ARTHUR   you already do. this is you. this is your shit.

PAUL   it's yours. not mine. you evil runt. i wish you'd never left your fucking field.

ARTHUR   you're not leaving me here. we haven't finished yet.

PAUL   this is a nightmare.

ARTHUR   good.

don't you leave me paul. i swear, you go back to her and you'll regret it. i'll make you pay.

PAUL   what more can you do to me you haven't done already?

ARTHUR   don't you leave me.

PAUL	you don't love me. you don't look after me.
ARTHUR	i swear paul. you go back to play happy families and i'll make sure everyone, fucking everyone i tell you… in paris, fucking brussels, here, you name it… i'll make sure everyone knows what you and the 'young villain rimbaud' have been getting up to.
PAUL	you won't.
ARTHUR	i'll tell them what the little girls have been getting up to. my cock in your mouth and your prick up my arse.
PAUL	it would ruin you too.
ARTHUR	innocent? you think this is what little girls do? fuck innocence. no one who thinks is innocent.
PAUL	you wouldn't dare.
ARTHUR	try me.
PAUL	no arthur / please…
ARTHUR	i don't believe it.
PAUL	arthur please / don't…
ARTHUR	what are you trying to do to me? just what are you trying to do to me?
PAUL	nothing. i'm not doing anything.
ARTHUR	why are you making me do this?
PAUL	i'm not.
ARTHUR	you are you nasty bastard.
PAUL	it's you. trying to destroy me.
ARTHUR	this is self-defence.
PAUL	i don't want to hurt you artie.
ARTHUR	and art. in defence of art. you'd see me die.

PAUL   no.

ARTHUR   you push me too hard paul. too hard.
                what choice do i have?

PAUL   i didn't mean / to...

ARTHUR   you can't go back to paris.

PAUL   no arthur.

ARTHUR   not ever.

PAUL   no.

ARTHUR   it's for your own good. i promise.
                it's only me knows who you really are.
                it's only me sees inside of you.

PAUL   i know.

ARTHUR   because i love you.

PAUL   i love you. i love you too.

ARTHUR   then say you're sorry.

PAUL   it's only because i don't feel well. i wouldn't
                do anything to hurt you artie.

ARTHUR   then say you're sorry.

PAUL   i'm sorry.

ARTHUR   you won't go.

PAUL   no.

                pause.

ARTHUR   it'll be fine you know. everything's going to
                be just fine.

PAUL   if you say so.

ARTHUR   i do.
                we can teach. we'll advertise. the london times.
                'lessons in the french tongue from literary
                gentlemen.'

'lessons de langue française de la part
d'hommes de lettres.'
how does that sound?
and your book is nearly finished. and that'll
make you feel better. and with the money
from your book and the teaching. maybe we
could have a little holiday. won't that be nice.
we'll be okay paul.

PAUL
i know artie.
i think i'd die without you. i think if you
weren't with me, i'd have to kill myself.

ARTHUR
well i'm here and i'm not going anywhere.
and neither are you.
we've got to finish what we started paul.
you and me.
together.

IV

ARTHUR   i'm hungry.

PAUL   so. i'm dying.

              pause.

ARTHUR   i said i'm hungry.

PAUL   go and get something to eat then.

ARTHUR   you go.

PAUL   –

ARTHUR   got no money.

PAUL   –

ARTHUR   paul.

PAUL   –

ARTHUR   it's your turn to do the shopping.

PAUL   –

ARTHUR   paul.

PAUL   jesus fucking christ.
              do i have to do everything in this fucking
              household?
              well get off me then.

              pointing to a bottle of gin.

              and don't you dare finish that off.
              idle peasant.

              ARTHUR *gives him the finger.*

              PAUL *leaves.*

              MODERNIST SCHISM

              [*what follows are some thoughts as to what
              might make a 'modernist schism' at this point
              in the performance.*]

              the actor playing ARTHUR…

              …announces the date and time

              *…passes a camera to a spectator and asks
              them to film him/her*

              *…writes 'EVER SEEN ANYTHING LIKE
              THIS BEFORE?' on his/her chest*

              *… sings patti smith and lenny kaye's 'rock n
              roll nigger'*

              *… looks every member of the audience in the
              eye and says:*

              'i am an animal, a savage.
              but i can be saved.

you are fake savages; maniacs, brutes, misers, the lot of you.'

… is dada

… is a cubist painting

… passes an iphone round playing a youtube clip of stravinsky's 'the rite of spring'

… dances like nijinsky

… holds up a series of signs some of which might say:

'NOUS NOUS EN FOUTONS…'
'… ET NOUS AVONS LE TEMPS'
'WE ARE YOUNG…'
'… AND WE DON'T GIVE A FUCK'
'WELCOME TO THE C20TH'
'ARE WE NEW YET?'

ARTHUR   rimbaud est mort. vive rimbaud.
l'art est mort. vive l'art.

                ARTHUR *has emptied the bottle.*

                il est où, putain.

                he goes to the window and leans out.

                oi. tu étais où, putain?
madame verlaine.
qu'est ce que tu as là?

(PAUL   piss off.)

                he is laughing.

ARTHUR   look at you. you look a right twat.
regardez le.
tu as l'air complètement con.
fucking ridiculous.
you fool.
connard.
what do you think you look like?

PAUL *enters*.

PAUL *has a dead fish in one hand and a bottle of oil in the other.*

pause.

mackerel.

PAUL *swings the fish at* ARTHUR, *hitting him on the side of the head.* ARTHUR *falls to the floor.*

PAUL   i do not look ridiculous.

PAUL *starts to pack belongings into a case.*

ARTHUR *comes round.*

ARTHUR   what are you doing?

PAUL   what does it look like halfwit?

ARTHUR   but why.
you're not leaving paul.
you can't go.

PAUL   that is precisely what i'm doing genius.

ARTHUR   you can't. paul. you can't go.

PAUL   watch me.

ARTHUR   don't go.

PAUL   i can't go on like this. this can't go on.

ARTHUR   i didn't mean it. you don't look ridiculous.

PAUL   this this violence.

ARTHUR   you / hit me.

PAUL   i'm exhausted.

ARTHUR *tries to get up and* PAUL *threatens him with the bottle of oil.*

don't try and stop me.

ARTHUR   you can't leave. not after everything i've done for you.

PAUL   done to me.

ARTHUR   the book. 'romances.' you finished your book.

PAUL   so now i can go.

ARTHUR   what will i do?

PAUL   i don't care.

ARTHUR   i'll starve.

PAUL   –

ARTHUR   but you love me.

PAUL   if i'm not back with mathilde in three days i'll shoot myself.

ARTHUR   you don't have a gun.

PAUL   i'll buy one. you try to stop me and i'll blow my fucking brains out arthur. you see if i won't.
it'll be your fault. your fault.

ARTHUR   but i've got nothing paul. nothing.

PAUL *throws his bag at* ARTHUR *and runs out of the room.*

PAUL   you've had everything.

ARTHUR   come back. come back.
come back you bastard.
you think it's going to be that easy.
i'll fucking show you.
you faggot.
pederast.

he leans out of the window.

pédé. him. there. pédé.
they'll be waiting for you. the police.

they'll be waiting.
no one does that to me.
fuck. fucking fuck.
shit. shit. shit.

Brussels

july 1873.

a cheap hotel.

this scene takes place inside and outside a room: fictionally, a communal bathroom off a corridor of this hotel.

bracketed speech indicates 'outside' the bathroom.

I

PAUL *enters.*

he is exceptionally, stupidly drunk.

he closes the door, dropping the key once or twice before locking it behind him.

he sits.

he takes a bottle of brandy from one pocket and a small pistol from another.

soft knocking.

PAUL	no one listens.
	more knocking.
	i know what's true.
(MATHILDE	paul?)
PAUL	no one wants to listen.
(MATHILDE	paul. are you in there?)

MATHILDE *rattles the door handle.*

PAUL   (*shouts*) mathilde.

(MATHILDE   (*to someone passing in the corridor*) good
                morning.)

PAUL   i said i'm sorry.

(MATHILDE   there are people paul.
                what will they think.
                please…)

PAUL   listen.

(MATHILDE   you're tired paul. why don't you come back to
                your room and rest.)

PAUL   take me home, mathilde.

                pause.

(MATHILDE   you'll feel better after a sleep. and then we
                can talk. so why don't you come out of there.)

PAUL   can't.

(MATHILDE   open the door paul.)

PAUL   i can't let him in he'll kill me.

(MATHILDE   sshhhh / please…)

PAUL   you can't leave me here.
                mathilde if you leave me here it's murder.
                / murder.

(MATHILDE   no you asked him to come.
                you wrote to him.)

PAUL   not true.

(MATHILDE   he showed me your letter.)

PAUL   he lies. he's lying. take me back mathilde.

(MATHILDE   come out paul.)

PAUL   no.

(MATHILDE	then let me in.)
PAUL	i can't let him in.
(MATHILDE	rimbaud's downstairs. i'm alone.)
PAUL	just you?
(MATHILDE	yes.)
PAUL	yes?
(MATHILDE	yes.)

PAUL *pulls on the door handle.*

PAUL	i can't.
(MATHILDE	yes you can.)
PAUL	i can't. won't open. locked.
(MATHILDE	how oh the key the key is in the door. unlock the door. with the key.)

as PAUL *unlocks the door,* MATHILDE *pushes it open, knocking* PAUL *backwards and the gun across the floor.*

he scrambles after the gun, picks it up and turns to MATHILDE*, pointing it at her.*

MATHILDE *screams.*

PAUL	no. shh. shh. shut up.

he points the gun to his own head.

look. it's for me. look.

MATHILDE	no you can't, not that. paul.
PAUL	take me back mathilde.
MATHILDE	you can't do that.
PAUL	i don't know what else to do.
MATHILDE	we can talk put the gun down.
PAUL	i can be better.

MATHILDE   we can be civilised put the gun down. i want
             us to be civilised.

             he rests the gun in his lap.

PAUL   okay. here. civilised.
             the door... you better... people can...

             she closes the door.

             i'm sick mathilde.
             take me home and make me better.

MATHILDE   let's go to your room.

PAUL   home. i want to go home. to paris

MATHILDE   i don't think that's a good idea.

PAUL   i want my family.

MATHILDE   there's no place for you in a family.

PAUL   there is. it's mine. my family.
             you're my wife. take me back.

MATHILDE   how can i be your wife. everyone knows
             about you and that... him.

PAUL   just gossip.

MATHILDE   it's against god. and nature.

PAUL   no?

MATHILDE   no.

             he holds the gun up to his head again.

             no. don't. you can't harm yourself. please no.

PAUL   you give me no choice.

MATHILDE   think of george.
             he hasn't hurt anyone. he's innocent.

PAUL   i'm innocent.

MATHILDE   please give me the gun.

PAUL   you'd leave me here with him. and nothing to
                protect myself with.
                you want me dead.

MATHILDE   no i don't i didn't say that. why is everything
                the opposite of how it's supposed to be with
                you.

PAUL   please mathilde please, i'm begging you
                please. he's here to kill me.

MATHILDE   for pity's sake, paul, you asked him to come.
                you asked him to bring your manuscripts.

PAUL   he's what?

MATHILDE   he has your papers. your letters.

PAUL   ha. see. i told you. didn't i say. you see.

MATHILDE   see what?

PAUL   innocent. my secretary. that's all. all he is.
                ammanu / myamman…

MATHILDE   it really doesn't matter. please / give me the…

PAUL   it does matter. where is he? why isn't he here?
                i want him here.

MATHILDE   why don't you / give me…

PAUL   bring him here.

MATHILDE   first the / gun.

PAUL   immediately. i want him here. tell him to
                come here.

MATHILDE   later per…

                PAUL *holds the gun up to his head again.*

                no paul please.

PAUL   get him. i'll prove it to you. get him here.
                now. run damn you.

he waves the gun at MATHILDE. *she yelps and runs out.*

PAUL *attempts to tidy himself up.*

i'll show you. it's all going to be fine. i'll sort this out.

all going to be fine.

ARTHUR *enters, holding* PAUL*'s case.*

ARTHUR	morning paul.
PAUL	morning arthur.
ARTHUR	how are you?
PAUL	very well, thank you.
ARTHUR	you're looking well i must say.
PAUL	–
ARTHUR	picture of domestic contentment.
PAUL	yes.
ARTHUR	reconciliation going well then. i mean old carrot-face looks delighted. really.
PAUL	we're very happy.
ARTHUR	brought your letters and stuff.
PAUL	where is she?
ARTHUR	your manuscripts.
PAUL	where's my wife?
ARTHUR	it's just you and me paul. man to man. don't think carrot-face's got the stomach for it.
PAUL	i know what you're up to.
ARTHUR	brought you this. all the way from london.
PAUL	it's not going to work.

ARTHUR	exactly like you asked.
PAUL	won't work.
ARTHUR	what won't?
PAUL	i'm not / coming back to…
ARTHUR	come back to london with me paul.
PAUL	no.
ARTHUR	it's no good without you.
PAUL	i can't.
ARTHUR	you can. you have to. what else you going to do? mathilde won't save you.
PAUL	she will.
ARTHUR	you're already overboard paul. give in to it.
PAUL	no.
ARTHUR	i'm all you've got. it's you and me at sea.
PAUL	you hurt me artie.
ARTHUR	and you hurt me. we're as bad as each other. but they're stupid arguments. that's all they are. we can stop. i can say i'm sorry. will you let me say i'm sorry? i'm sorry paul.
PAUL	i can't live like you.
ARTHUR	we'll be nice to each other. i can make you feel better. i can.
PAUL	no.
ARTHUR	who'll hold you paul. who's going to put their arms around you. feel the weight of you.

PAUL	–
ARTHUR	no one. only me. it's me you need not her. you don't belong in her world.
PAUL	it's the only one there is. there's nothing else.
ARTHUR	you're only free with me.
PAUL	i don't need free.
ARTHUR	that's not true.
PAUL	you don't need me.
ARTHUR	but we haven't finished.
PAUL	look… (*pointing to the case*) in there. that's it. there's nothing more.
ARTHUR	what about our new church.
PAUL	i'm only a poet.
ARTHUR	you promised.
PAUL	i can't.
ARTHUR	you cunt.
PAUL	sshhh.
ARTHUR	you what?
PAUL	ssshhhh. other people. people will hear.
ARTHUR	fucking what you cunt. / 'people will hear.' too fucking right they will. let the fuckers hear this.
PAUL	ssshh. no. please. i didn't mean that…
ARTHUR	a fucking cock with a cunt. / that's what you are. that's what paul verlaine is. a cock with a cunt.
PAUL	no please don't. mathilde / mathilde …
ARTHUR	you're going to crawl back to that frigid imbecile?

PAUL   shut up. she'll hear you.

ARTHUR   her and every other bugger.
                listen up brussels. paul verlaine.
                / husband father gentleman poet...
                he fucks men.

PAUL   no. don't. arthur. stop it.

ARTHUR   been fucking me for the last two years and
                i'm not the first. what do you make of that
                brussels. what will paris make of it.

PAUL   please stop.

ARTHUR   i'll go to paris paul and i'll shout it from the
                fucking rooftops.

PAUL   please arthur.

ARTHUR   listen hypocrites. listen to the fucking truth.
                verlaine shits on you paris. he shits on you
                then he cries like a girl and he asks you to
                take him back.
                he despises you. and he fucks me. and he
                loves me. and he loves shit. and nothing you
                know means anything any more.
                that's the truth. that's art. that's verlaine.

PAUL   why are you doing this to me.

ARTHUR   we were going to change the world. you said.
                you said we're the real thing.

PAUL   i know...

ARTHUR   you're going back to mathilde?

PAUL   i have to.

ARTHUR   you're really going back to her?

PAUL   yes.

ARTHUR   yeah? yeah?
                then give me some fucking money.
                you went and left me with nothing you shit.

PAUL	i don't have any.
ARTHUR	give me some money. or i'm going to the police.
PAUL	please no please…
	PAUL *is blocking* ARTHUR*'s exit.*
	ARTHUR *throws the case at* PAUL.
ARTHUR	you spineless, witless apology for a poet. you fucking fake. i should get something for being your whore.
PAUL	you'll ruin both of us.
ARTHUR	you think you can fuck me for free?
PAUL	i don't have anything.
ARTHUR	then piss off out of my way.
	PAUL *waves the gun.*
PAUL	i'm warn…
	PAUL *fires the gun twice hitting* ARTHUR *in the hand.*
ARTHUR	fuck.
PAUL	artie.
ARTHUR	what have you done?
PAUL	are you alright?
ARTHUR	you shot me. you shot me.
PAUL	i didn't mean it.
ARTHUR	you fucking shot me.
	knocking on the door.
(MATHILDE	paul. paul. are you alright?)
ARTHUR	he fucking shot me.
(MATHILDE	are you alive paul?)

PAUL	i love you.
(MATHILDE	let me in.)
ARTHUR	you really shot me.
PAUL	i love you.
	MATHILDE *pushes the door open, which propels* PAUL *towards* ARTHUR.
ARTHUR	stay away from me, you bastard.
	PAUL *falls to the floor.*
MATHILDE	paul. are you all right?
PAUL	i don't feel well.
ARTHUR	it's me. me. he shot me.
MATHILDE	paul?
	PAUL *vomits.*
	oh.
	she closes the door.
ARTHUR	look. blood. fucking hell.
MATHILDE	(*to* ARTHUR) be quiet. paul.
PAUL	help me.
ARTHUR	i'm bleeding. that's my blood.
MATHILDE	yes, i can see that / mr rimbaud.
ARTHUR	he did this. him. your husband.
MATHILDE	he's / not my husband.
PAUL	what's going to / happen to me?
ARTHUR	he really shot me. it hurts.
PAUL	i'm so sorry. don't leave me mathilde.
ARTHUR	he's mad.

PAUL	what's happening?
MATHILDE	paul, sit / down.
ARTHUR	what about me? look at me. (*to* PAUL... *he goes to kick him*) cunt.
MATHILDE	let me see.
	she goes to ARTHUR.
ARTHUR	he could've fucking killed me.
PAUL	i want to die.
MATHILDE	(*to* ARTHUR) i don't think you're going to die.
ARTHUR	he's a lunatic. he should be locked up. (*to* PAUL) nutter. i'm going to the police.
MATHILDE	please don't do that.
ARTHUR	why? why not? look what he did to me.
MATHILDE	please spare me that. here.
	MATHILDE *takes his hand.*
ARTHUR	(*shouting*) ow.
MATHILDE	it's nothing serious. if i can just bandage it...
ARTHUR	it really hurts.
	she uses a handkerchief to bandage ARTHUR*'s wrist.*
PAUL	my angel.
ARTHUR	he should be locked up.
MATHILDE	hold still.
PAUL	look. you're an angel. you can look after both of us. mathilde. we could live together. i'm so sorry arthur. dear arthur.

MATHILDE   oh shut up paul.

PAUL   the three of us.
we can live together. brussels. london.
anywhere.
mathilde…

MATHILDE   how could you how could you even think
that.
it's beyond / beyond…

ARTHUR   i want money.

PAUL   we can do / what we want.
anything.

ARTHUR   or i'll go to the police.

MATHILDE   for my son's sake.

ARTHUR   i'll go to paris.
to the police in paris.

MATHILDE   please. i really don't think it's in anyone's
interest to be going to the police. here or in
paris.

ARTHUR   i need money.

MATHILDE   it's not so bad. i'm sure it will heal in no time.
if you keep pressing / on it…

ARTHUR   or the police.

MATHILDE   yes. well. as you've been so good as to return
paul's documents in person then i'm sure it's
appropriate to offer you the train fare home.

she takes some notes from her bag.

there must be enough there to see you home
to your own family.

he takes the money.

it's everything i have with me.

ARTHUR	paul. see.
	he is holding out the money.
	one last chance paul.
MATHILDE	what are you doing?
ARTHUR	we can start again.
MATHILDE	no that's not right.
ARTHUR	paul? we can go back to london. it's your last chance.
	PAUL *shakes his head.*
	you'll regret this.
MATHILDE	why what are you doing.
ARTHUR	i'll see you in hell.
	ARTHUR *leaves.*
PAUL	what's happening?
MATHILDE	i don't know.
PAUL	where's he going?
MATHILDE	i think he's going to the police.
PAUL	he's gone.
MATHILDE	shit.
PAUL	–
MATHILDE	give me that.
PAUL	we can be together now.
MATHILDE	paul.
PAUL	you can't leave me.
	he holds the gun up to his head.
	or i'll do it.

MATHILDE	it's too late.
PAUL	you can't divorce me.
MATHILDE	it's too late.
PAUL	it's not allowed.
MATHILDE	a court pronounced our separation six weeks ago. we were divorced six weeks ago.
PAUL	not true. not you. not you little carrot fairy.
MATHILDE	i'm not your carrot fairy any more.
PAUL	carrot fairy. mouse princess.
MATHILDE	stop it paul.
PAUL	i'll do anything.
MATHILDE	then give me that. please. george has done nothing to deserve this. he's a child. your child.
PAUL	i don't want to die.
MATHILDE	you can't take your own life paul. here's a word i've learnt… 'unconscionable'. it's unconscionable.
PAUL	i know.
MATHILDE	how could you? threaten us with that?
PAUL	i'm sorry.
MATHILDE	there's nothing inside you there's nothing holding you together.
PAUL	i can't do it. i'm so sorry. i'm pathetic i'm sorry.
MATHILDE	pathetic and sick and dirty and drunk and weak.
PAUL	then you do it. i don't want to live. please you do it.

he tries to press the gun into her hands.

MATHILDE   oh paul. may god forgive you.

he drops the gun.

daddy was right. you have no moral fibre.

PAUL   oh fuck your father.

she starts to pick up the documents scattered about the room, picking up the gun on her way.

no no i didn't mean it…

MATHILDE   i'm so ashamed.

PAUL   mathilde.

he tries to take hold of her hand.

MATHILDE   don't touch me.

PAUL   help me.

she is selecting documents to put back into the case and dropping others into a bin.

MATHILDE   i am helping you.

PAUL   what am i going to do?
tell me, please.

MATHILDE   –

PAUL   i don't want to be alone.

MATHILDE   how can someone like you write poetry.
i don't understand.

PAUL   what are you doing?

MATHILDE   clearing up this mess.

PAUL   what are you doing to my work.

MATHILDE   your work's safe. pass me that bottle paul.

he hands her the bottle of brandy.

PAUL	my letters.
MATHILDE	do you have any matches paul?
PAUL	letters from arthur.
MATHILDE	matches. do you have any? quickly. before the police get here.
PAUL	there are poems he wrote for me.
MATHILDE	i don't care. they're disgusting. it's all disgusting.

PAUL *has matches in his hand*.

PAUL	what are you doing to them.

*as she speaks she pours brandy into the bin
taking care to leave some in the bottle for*
PAUL.

MATHILDE	i married you before god and i'll always be your wife, whatever the court says. wife of the poet paul verlaine. no one should read these. not the police not george not anyone. i don't want anyone else to know this. i won't be remembered for this.

*she holds the brandy in one hand and the
other out for the matches*.

give me the matches.

PAUL *trades the brandy for the matches. he
drinks*.

MATHILDE *lights a match and throws it into
the bin, setting fire to the letters*.

PAUL	(*laughing and clapping*) bravo carrot-face. bravo. you have an imagination after all.
MATHILDE	you're sick paul.

PAUL   i know. i know i'm sick.

                MATHILDE *is at the door.*

MATHILDE   if rimbaud has gone to the police then perhaps
                you should think about leaving here sooner
                rather than later.

PAUL   forgive me.

MATHILDE   it's not for me to forgive what you've done.
                be careful paul.

                she leaves and closes the door behind her.

PAUL   it's dark. it's too dark.

                he kneels and prays.

                he has difficulty remembering the words.

                hail mary full of grace, the lord is with thee.
                blessed are thou among women and blessed is
                the fruit of thy womb jesus.
                holy mary
                mother of god, pray for me
                come to me
                let me see your face.

                the end.

A Nick Hern Book

slope first published in Great Britain in 2014 as a single edition paperback by Nick Hern Books Limited, The Glasshouse, 49a Goldhawk Road, London W12 8QP, in association with Untitled Projects

slope copyright © 2014 pamela carter

pamela carter has asserted her moral right to be identified as the author of this work

Cover photograph by Tobias Feltus

Designed and typeset by Nick Hern Books, London
Printed in Great Britain by Mimeo Ltd, Huntingdon, Cambridgeshire PE29 6XX

A CIP catalogue record for this book is available from the British Library

ISBN 978 1 84842 459 3

www.nickhernbooks.co.uk

 facebook.com/nickhernbooks

 twitter.com/nickhernbooks